RIVER RESCUE

by Jennifer Keats Curtis and
Tri-State Bird Rescue & Research, Inc.
illustrated by Tammy Yee

On shore, two big pelicans hop rather than fly. See how black their bellies are? They are covered with oil. They cannot fly, and they cannot swim.

Water birds—like pelicans, swans, herons, ducks, and geese—have special feathers that lock together like Velcro® to create a waterproof drysuit.

A drysuit is a protective suit worn by people working or playing in cold water. The suit keeps water out and the wearer warm and dry.

Droplets of water bead up and roll off the feathery drysuit. Without waterproofing, water penetrates that layer. The pelicans become cold and wet. They cannot get off the ground, and they cannot float. When they use their beaks to preen—clean and straighten their feathers—they will swallow the oil on their feathers. This can make them sick.

Oil spills affect many animals, not just pelicans. Everything that lives in and near the water—salamanders, crayfish, frogs, newts, turtles, dragonflies, and horseshoe crabs—can become coated with oil. Like birds, they too can become sick. They may die.

Sometimes oil spills are huge, but it doesn't take much oil to affect water and animals. Think about how one drop of oil on the water quickly spreads over a large surface. And, it's not just oil that spills from ships or energy plants that can affect animals. Diesel fuel, gasoline, jet fuel, and even cooking oil can leak into the environment and hurt wildlife.

Workers rush to the scene to clean the water and shoreline. Who cleans the animals?

We do. We are the Oiled Wildlife Response Team at Tri-State Bird Rescue & Research in Delaware. Only a few organizations in the United States can save these animals. Tri-State is the only experienced team on the East Coast.

When we get a call to help, we rush to the scene. We pick up as many oiled animals as we can, capturing some with nets.

We drive them to Tri-State so that we can treat them as quickly as possible. In our "Emergency Room," vets and assistants examine the animals to determine how sick they are and the best ways to take care of them. Oil can be dangerous for people too, so we wear suits and gloves to protect ourselves.

These are wild animals, and they don't want to be here. They don't feel well and are probably afraid of people.

When an animal arrives, we carefully examine him. What kind of animal is he? How old is he?

Is he active and alert or tired and weak? What kind of oil is on him? Is it all over him or just in spots? We carefully check all parts of his body, including the inside of his mouth. We check his breathing. Is it slow or fast? Is he wheezing?

After the exam, we decide how to treat him. We might gently slide a tube into his stomach to give him clear fluids and medicine to protect his insides from the oil.

We flush his eyes and clean his mouth and nostrils. We make sure the animals we are caring for are warm in the winter and cool in the summer. If they become too hot or too cold, they could die.

The only way to help is to get the oil off. To do this, we have to wash and rinse them.

Washing and rinsing can take a long time and requires many helpers. We may have to use six tubs, each with a different amount of detergent in the tub.

With birds, we move them from tub to tub until all the oil comes off. We use gentle tools, like soft toothbrushes and cotton swabs, to help remove the oil. Birds' normal body temperature is 104°F (40°C) so we wash and rinse them in water heated to that temperature.

In many cases, it takes two or three people to handle the bird for 30 minutes or more of washing. One holds the bird and one or two wash him, making sure soap does not get into his eyes or mouth. Another group rinses the bird. That can take another 30 minutes or longer. We try to get the oil off in one wash and rinse. When water beads up and rolls off the bird's feathers, we know he is clean and his waterproofing process can begin. We then dry him with heat lamps and blowers, just like those used to dry dogs and cats. It can take up to two hours for the bird to dry, depending on how thick his feathers are and if he is preening.

We have to know a lot about these animals to properly care for them. For birds, we need to know if they live by themselves or in a flock. Do they spend most of their time in the water? Can they walk on land? We must feed them what they eat in the wild, so we must know what they eat and how they find food. Do they migrate? When and where?

If the bird is used to a flock, like a Mallard or Canada goose, he goes into an area with other birds. Loons and grebes prefer to be alone. They are housed by themselves. And, since they are diving birds, their feet are quite far back on their bodies. They don't really walk. In the wild, they only get out of the water to incubate eggs. They must go into a pen that has mesh on the bottom, like a hammock, to support their bodies and keep them comfortable.

Once the bird is dry, he goes into a clean pen with food and water. We will spray him lightly with water several times a day to make sure his feathers are waterproofed. He will keep preening to get his feathers back in place. In a couple of days, we move him to an outside cage with a pool if it's warm enough. If it is too cold, we set up a pool inside. We give the birds time to swim and preen to make sure they are waterproof.

It can take days or a week for the birds to become waterproofed and well enough to be released. When they are ready to go, we place a metal band around one of their legs. The bands have numbers on them so that we can identify the birds in the future.

We hope to return these animals to the same spot where they were captured. We can only do this if the site is clean of oil. Otherwise, we may have to find another place nearby for release.

Our favorite part of this process is the release. A duck flies home, a heron returns to his river, a turtle scoots back into his pond. We hope we won't see them again, but if they need us, we'll be here.

For Creative Minds

Preventing Oil Spills & Helping Animals

People hear "oil spill" and usually think of an oil pipeline that breaks or a rig or ship spewing black, shiny oil that floats across water and onto the land. While that is one kind of oil spill, other fuels and even cooking oil can quickly spread across water and the shores. Any kind of oil spill can hurt animals that live in and near water. Oil ruins animals' ability to insulate or waterproof themselves. Oil-covered animals become cold and waterlogged. They may swallow the oil, which makes them sick.

After an oil spill, trained responders come with tools to soak up, clean up, vacuum, and move the oil. How the oil is cleaned will depend on what kind of oil has spilled, how much there is, where the oil has spilled and the time of year.

Even in our own homes, we can help prevent oil spill problems by:
- Putting lids on items that contain any kind of oil or grease, even peanut butter, before we throw them away.
- Disposing of cooking oil the right way—let it cool and put it in a container with a lid.
- Never dump any kind of oil outside or into the garbage or sewer.
- Checking and maintaining inside and outside oil tanks because they can rust and leak.
- Thinking about how we can use less oil, such as riding our bikes, walking or carpooling rather than taking our car.
- Remembering to turn off the lights and unplug electronic devices, like TVs and computers, when they are not in use. Using less electricity means using less oil.

Besides oil, trash can also hurt wildlife. How can you help animals stay free from pollution?
- When you see trash, pick it up and put it in a recycling bin or trash can with the lid on so that no animals will become tangled in it or take it back to their homes. Fishing line, kite strings, balloons, and plastic bags are especially dangerous trash.
- Rethink the ways you use plastic and reduce the amount of trash you produce. Pack your lunch in reusable containers rather than plastic bags. Use a reusable water bottle.
- Organize a clean-up day around your home or school.
- Ask your principal about a recycling program at your school if one isn't already in place.

Wildlife Identification

Oil spills can affect every animal that lives in and near the water. Can you identify these animals that were helped at Tri-State?

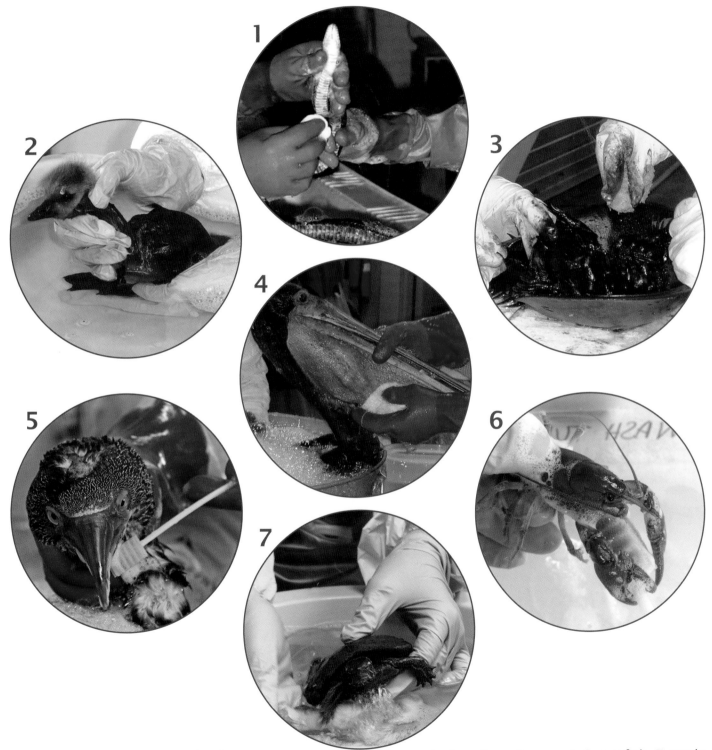

Answers: 1. snake, 2. young goose, 3. horseshoe crab, 4, pelican, 5. gannet, 6. crayfish, 7. turtle

Q&A with Tri-State Executive Director Lisa Smith

How often do you rescue oiled animals?
We never know when oil spills will occur or if animals will be affected, so we remain ready all of the time.

What was the biggest spill that you've been involved in?
The 2010 spill in the Gulf of Mexico. We set up treatment centers in Louisiana, Mississippi, Alabama, and Florida. We cared for over 2,000 birds. Brown Pelicans were the most common patient.

What is the hardest animal to clean and why?
Each animal presents challenges. Pelicans can be tricky. They often get oil inside their pouches. That has to be carefully cleaned. Diving birds like loons have very dense feathers so it can take longer to wash them the right way. Diving birds are also hard to clean because they can't stand like geese and ducks. We put them in special cages where the bottom looks like a hammock. We work hard to get them clean and into pools as fast as possible.

What is the biggest animal you have helped? The smallest?
The biggest have been beavers and snapping turtles that weigh over 50 pounds! The smallest have been songbirds, tiny turtles, frogs, salamanders, and crayfish.

How much does it cost to care for oiled animals?
It depends on the circumstances, but it is expensive. We need many experienced people but professional treatment increases the chances of the animals returning to the wild, so it's worth it. Other costs include:
- The right food, like fish for pelicans
- Medical supplies and safety equipment, such as special suits and gloves
- Getting rid of oily wastewater collected during washing
- Fuel to heat hot water for washing.

You want the animals in your care to stay as wild as possible so that they can be released. Do the animals get attached to you?
No, we try not to talk around them or to them. We make sure we never treat them like pets. We want them to go back to the wild where they belong.

How hard is it to catch animals affected by oil?
It depends on the type of oil and how much is on the animals. If the oil is heavy, like crude oil, the animals are often easy to catch. They can't fly or run away. If the oil is light, like diesel fuel, they can be hard to catch. They may still be able to fly or get away. Sometimes, we use special traps or cannon nets to catch oiled birds that can still fly.

Who cares for the animals?
Most of our staff have a background in biology or animal science. They have volunteered at Tri-State or worked in places like Tri-State. Our wildlife veterinarian has very special qualifications. Some staff members are veterinary technicians. Staff or volunteers who will be working with mammals (like raccoons) must have pre-exposure rabies vaccinations so they can safely handle these animals.

What is the best part of your job?
One is seeing how many people care about wildlife and how hard they will work to help them. The other is returning animals to their wild homes once their rehabilitation is complete.

What should I do if I find an oiled animal?
Call a licensed wildlife rehabilitator. Every wild animal is different. If you aren't experienced in handling these animals, you could be hurt or they could be hurt. Oil can be dangerous for people. Don't touch it with your bare hands. Latex gloves will not protect you from some unsafe substances. If you see an oil spill, please call the National Response Center at (800) 424-8802.

Thanks to Lisa Smith of Tri-State Bird Rescue & Research for verifying the accuracy of the information in this book.

Photo credits go to Tri-State Bird Rescue & Research and to the EXXON VALDEZ Oil Spill Trustee Council for the images used in the For Creative Minds section.

Library of Congress Cataloging-in-Publication Data

Names: Curtis, Jennifer Keats, author. | Yee, Tammy, illustrator. | Tri-State
    Bird Rescue & Research, author, photographer.
Title: River rescue / by Jennifer Keats Curtis and Tri-State Bird Rescue &
    Research, Inc. ; illustrated by Tammy Yee.
Description: Mt. Pleasant, SC : Arbordale Publishing, [2020] | Audience: Age
    4-9. | Audience: K to Grade 3. | Includes bibliographical references. |
    Description based on print version record and CIP data provided by
    publisher; resource not viewed.
Identifiers: LCCN 2018040514 (print) | LCCN 2018049052 (ebook) | ISBN
    9781607188766 (English PDF) | ISBN 9781643511573 (English ePub) | ISBN
    9781607188797 (Interactive, read-aloud ebook English) | ISBN
    9781607188230 (english hardcover) | ISBN 9781607188353 (english paperback)
Subjects: LCSH: Oil spills and wildlife--Juvenile literature. | Birds--Effect
    of oil spills on--Juvenile literature.
Classification: LCC QH545.O5 (ebook) | LCC QH545.O5 C88 2020 (print) | DDC
    363.738/2--dc23
LC record available at https://lccn.loc.gov/2018040514

Lexile® Level: 820L
key phrases: environmental education, helping animals, oil spills

Bibliography
Benoit, Peter. The Exxon Valdez Oil Spill. Children's Press, 2011. Print
"Journey of an Oiled Juvenile Northern Gannet." YouTube, YouTube, 21 Jan. 2016, Internet
MiamiHerald. "Saving Louisiana's Wildlife One Pelican at a Time." YouTube, YouTube, 26 May 2010. Internet
"Ohio Spill Patient Release." YouTube, YouTube, 10 Dec. 2015. Internet
Lisa Smith, Executive Director, Tri-State Bird Rescue & Research; personal interview, multiple 2016 and 2017

Manufactured in China, December 2018
This product conforms to CPSIA 2008
First Printing

Arbordale Publishing
Mt. Pleasant, SC 29464
www.ArbordalePublishing.com